Facts About Countries
Spain

Ian Graham

SEA-TO-SEA
Mankato Collingwood London

Welcome to Spain

Spain is in the southwestern corner of Europe. It also controls the Balearic Islands in the Mediterranean Sea and the Canary Islands in the Atlantic Ocean.

Borders and coasts

Spain borders Portugal, France, Gibraltar, and the tiny state of Andorra. It almost touches Africa in the south. With three, long coastlines, Spain is one of the most popular places for beach vacations.

Below. **Calle Alcalá, one of the main streets in the capital city, Madrid.**

ATLANTIC OCEAN

Bay of Biscay

Golfe de Gascogne

FRANCE

44°N

La Coruña
Santiago de Compostela
Oviedo
Gijón
Santander
Bilbao
San Sebastián
CORDILLERA
Villablino
Vitoria
Pamplona
ANDORRA
PYRENEES
Golfe du Lion
42°N
Vigo
Orense
SIERRA CABRERA
León
Logroño
Figueres
Gerona
COSTA BRAVA
Esla
Burgos
SISTEMA IBERICO
Zaragoza
Ebro
Lérida
Tarrasa
Barcelona
Valladolid
Duero
Zamora
Tarragona
Salamanca
Segovia
Guadalajara
40°N
Menorca
Mallorca
Palma
MADRID
S P A I N
Tajo
Toledo
MESETA CENTRAL
Valencia
Júcar
Ibiza
BALEARIC ISLANDS
Cáceres
Trujillo
MONTES DE TOLEDO
Albacete
Alcira
Ibiza
Badajoz
Guadiana
Ciudad Real
Alcoy
Formentera
38°N
Puertollano
Alcaráz
Alicante
Nerva
SIERRA MORENA
Guadalquivir
Linares
SIERRA DE SEGURA
Murcia
Córdoba
Martos
Lorca
Cartagena
Huelva
Sevilla
Granada
Cerro de Mulhacén
Almería
Antequera
SIERRA NEVADA
Golfo de Cadiz
Jerez de la Frontera
Málaga
Marbella
COSTA DEL SOL
36°N
Cádiz
Gibraltar
Strait of Gibraltar
Ceuta
MEDITERRANEAN
ALGERIA
Melilla
34°N

PORTUGAL

MOROCCO

N
W   E
S

CANARY ISLANDS

La Palma
Santa Cruz de La Palma
Tenerife
Santa Cruz de Tenerife
Lanzarote
Arrecife
Fuerteventura
Puerto del Rosario
Gomera
Teide
Las Palmas
Hierro
Gran Canaria

Mountains   △ Mountain peak
Grassland and farmland
☐ Capital   ○ Major city
Country boundary

0   200 Miles

0   200 Kilometers

8°W   6°W   4°W   2°W   0°   2°E

The Land

The middle of Spain is a wide, flat area called the Meseta Central. Around this plateau there are high mountains.

Mountains and rivers

The Pyrénées Mountains in the north separate Spain and France. Other high mountain ranges include the Cordillera Cantabrica in the north and the Sierra Nevada in the south. Several large rivers, including the Tajo, flow from the mountains across Spain to the sea.

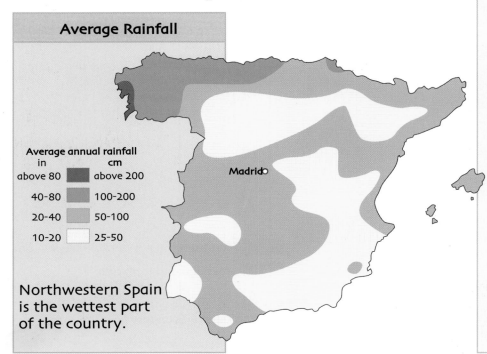

Average Rainfall

Average annual rainfall	
in	cm
above 80	above 200
40-80	100-200
20-40	50-100
10-20	25-50

Madrid

Northwestern Spain is the wettest part of the country.

Wildlife

Spain has many different plants and animals. It is so close to Africa that some African plants and animals survive here.

Mammals:
European wolf, brown bear, barbary ape (in Gibraltar), wild boar, wild goat, red deer, Egyptian mongoose, blind mole, red squirrel, dormouse, weasel, bat, rabbit, fox, and monk seal.

Birds:
Golden eagle, black vulture, peregrine falcon, marsh harrier, woodpecker, eagle owl, barn owl, buzzard, red kite, white stork, golden oriole, and pheasant.

Reptiles and amphibians:
Gecko, marbled newt, fire salamander, ocellated lizard, smooth snake, whip snake, green treefrog, and chameleon.

Above. A village in the mountains near the east coast of Spain. Here the land is very dry during the hot summer.

Climate

Spain is so big that different regions have different climates. Northern Spain is close to the Atlantic Ocean and has a mild, wet climate. Along the Mediterranean coast it is hotter and more humid. The Meseta Central is cooler and drier than the coast in winter. In summer it is very hot and dry.

Island climate

The Canary Islands are off the coast of North Africa. On these islands it is hot all year round. On the Balearic Islands it is mild in winter and hot and dry in summer.

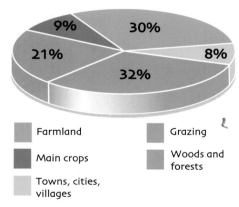

Farmland — 9%
Grazing — 30%
Main crops — 21%
Woods and forests — 8%
Towns, cities, villages — 32%

Above. How the land is used in Spain. A lot of the land is too hilly or too dry to grow crops.

7

The People

About 40 million people live in Spain. They are descendants of many different groups of people who have invaded and settled in Spain over the past 2,500 years.

Different kingdoms

The Celts, Basques, and Ancient Greeks have all invaded Spain. Spain was a patchwork of different kingdoms until about 230 B.C.E. After this, the Romans conquered all the kingdoms of Spain. After the Romans, the Visigoths invaded from Germany and the Moors from North Africa. Spain only became one country again in the fifteenth century.

Language

Almost everyone in Spain speaks the country's main language, Castilian. Each region is allowed to have its own language. These include Catalan, Basque, Galician, and Aragonese.

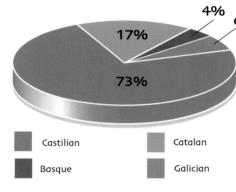

17%   4%   6%

73%

- Castilian
- Basque
- Catalan
- Galician

Above. **Main languages spoken in Spain.**

Below. **A stand selling fruit and vegetables in Málaga, in southern Spain.**

Above. Traditional Spanish dancing in a square in Las Palmas. The town is on Gran Canaria, one of the Canary Islands.

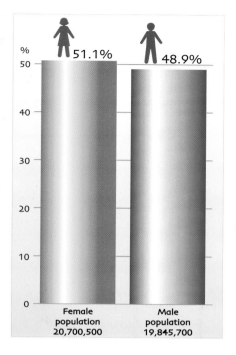

Female population 20,700,500	51.1%
Male population 19,845,700	48.9%

Above. The numbers of men and women in Spain.

Population

Most people live in Madrid and along the eastern and southern coasts.

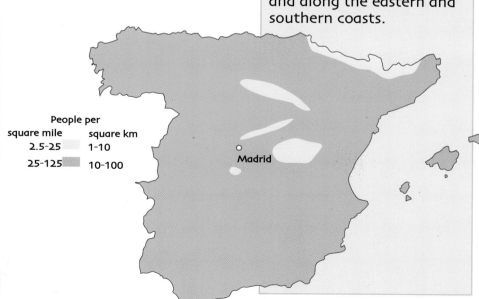

People per
square mile   square km
   2.5-25   1-10
   25-125   10-100

Madrid

Web Search ▶▶

▶ www.in-spain.info/
All about Spain and its people.

▶ http://encarta.msn.com/
fact_631504865/Spain_
Facts_and_Figures.html
Population figures for all countries, including Spain.

Town and Country Life

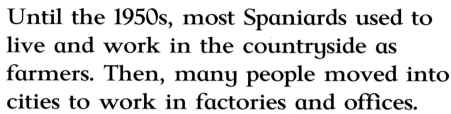

Until the 1950s, most Spaniards used to live and work in the countryside as farmers. Then, many people moved into cities to work in factories and offices.

Becoming richer

Today, more than 75 percent of Spain's population live in towns and cities. Most Spaniards have a better lifestyle than ever before. Some of them are wealthier than many other Europeans. But many people still living in the countryside in the south and west of Spain are among the poorest people in Europe.

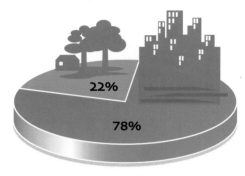

22%

78%

■ Percentage of population living in towns and cities

■ Percentage of population living in the country

Above. **Where people live.**

Back in Time

The first people arrived in Spain 35,000 years ago. They lived along the coast. In about 5000 B.C.E., they were joined by people from North Africa. In about 1500 B.C.E., people spread from the coast inland. By C.E. 500, there were towns and villages all over the country.

Right. **All the houses in this village are made of stone and have red, tiled roofs.**

Busy cities

Spanish cities are crowded and noisy. The streets are often jammed with traffic. At night, the city streets are still busy because people go out for the evening.

Quiet villages

Life in the villages is slower and more peaceful than in the towns. The streets are narrow but there is less traffic. The buildings are smaller. Instead of supermarkets, villages mostly have small shops and street markets.

Web Search ►►

► https://www.cia.gov/
library/publications/
the-world-factbook/
index.html
Information about Spain,
its people, government,
industry, and economy.

Farming and Fishing

Fewer people work on the land than they used to. However, farming is still important in Spain. So, too, is fishing.

Family farms

Most of Spain's farms are small compared to those in other countries in Western Europe. Most farms are owned and run by families. They grow mainly cereal crops, such as wheat, barley, and rice.

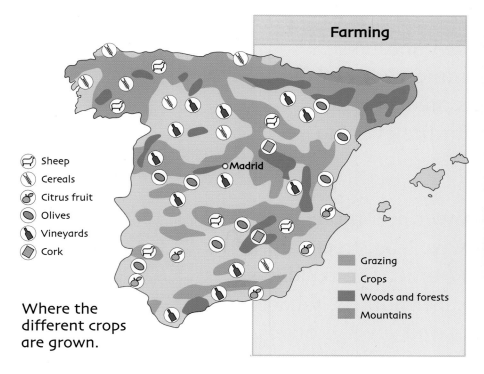

Farming

Sheep
Cereals
Citrus fruit
Olives
Vineyards
Cork

○Madrid

Grazing
Crops
Woods and forests
Mountains

Where the different crops are grown.

Above. **Melons are grown under plastic in Almería on the southern coast.**

Commercial Fishing

Spanish people eat more fish than people in any other European country. Spain has 18,900 fishing boats— more than all the other countries in Europe put together.

Left. **Selling fresh fish in Santa Pola, a small town on the east coast.**

🌐 **Web Search** ▶▶

▶ **www.fao.org**
Fishing in Spain.

▶ **http://countrystudies.us/ spain/**
Farming and fishing.

Wine, olives and fruit

Spain is one of the world's biggest wine makers. Rioja is Spain's best-known wine. Spanish sherry from the Jerez de la Frontera region is world famous. Spain has huge areas of olive trees. Most of the olives are used to make olive oil. The warm climate in the south of Spain is also perfect for growing tomatoes and oranges.

Below. **Main crops grown.**

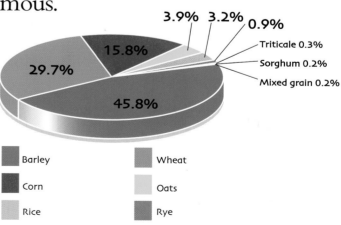

3.9% 3.2% 0.9%
Triticale 0.3%
Sorghum 0.2%
Mixed grain 0.2%
15.8%
29.7%
45.8%

- Barley
- Corn
- Rice
- Wheat
- Oats
- Rye

Resources and Industry

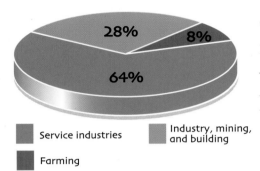

28%

8%

64%

Service industries

Industry, mining, and building

Farming

Above. **Workers in industry.**

Spain is rich in many metals, including mercury, nickel, lead, copper, and uranium. It has a lot of coal but very little oil or natural gas.

Industry

Making cars, trucks, and tractors is Spain's biggest manufacturing industry. Spanish car factories produce about 3 million cars a year, most of which are sold to other European countries.

The building industry is also important in Spain. Companies build hotels, homes, schools, and offices. Ships are also built in Spain, but the shipbuilding industry is not as important as the clothing industry. About one-tenth of Spain's factory workers work in textile and clothing factories.

Left. **A marble quarry. Marble is used in buildings, often as flooring.**

Service industry

As in many other European countries, most Spanish people work in service industries. They work mainly in tourism, insurance, and banking, selling goods, telecommunications, and transportation.

Right. An oil tanker docks at an oil refinery on the southeastern coast.

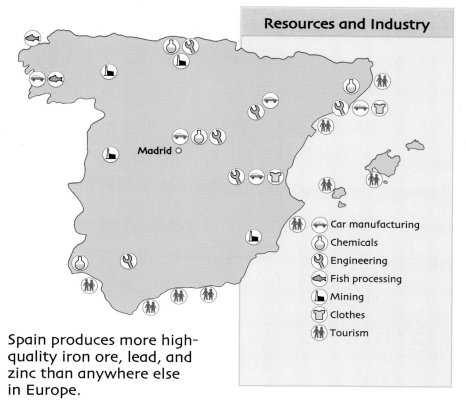

Resources and Industry

Madrid

Car manufacturing
Chemicals
Engineering
Fish processing
Mining
Clothes
Tourism

Spain produces more high-quality iron ore, lead, and zinc than anywhere else in Europe.

Web Search ▶▶

▶ http://minerals.usgs.gov/
Production of minerals and mining in different countries, including Spain.

▶ http://minerals.usgs.gov/
minerals/pubs/country/
2000/9438000.pdf
A mineral map of Spain.

▶ www.eia.doe.gov/emeu/cabs/
spain.html
Spanish energy industry.

Transportation

It is easy to travel around Spain because there are plenty of main roads, a good railroad network, and many airports.

Roads

Most of Spain's highways join Madrid and the other big cities such as Valencia, Cádiz, Vigo, Bilbao, and Barcelona. Buses take people, and trucks carry goods between cities and towns and to the smallest villages.

Speed Limits

The speed limit on Spain's highways is 75mph (120km/h). On other roads, it is either 55mph (90km/h) or 60mph (100km/h). In built-up areas, the speed limit is 30mph (50km/h).

Below. **This ferry carries people and cars to and from the Balearic Islands.**

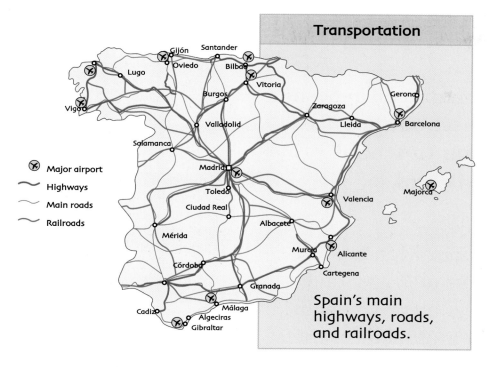

Transportation

Spain's main highways, roads, and railroads.

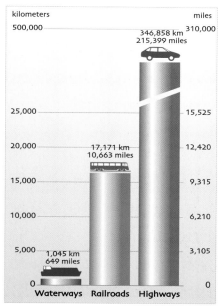

kilometers		miles
500,000		310,000

346,858 km
215,399 miles

25,000 — 15,525

20,000 — 12,420
17,171 km
10,663 miles

15,000 — 9,315

10,000 — 6,210

5,000 — 3,105
1,045 km
649 miles

0 — 0

Waterways   Railroads   Highways

Above. Spain's road, railroad, and waterway networks. Waterways are rivers and canals that are used by boats and barges.

Railways

Trains carry people and goods between cities and towns. There are fast, long-distance trains, regional trains, and trains for people who live in the countryside but work in the cities. Spain's railroad network links to railroads in France and Portugal.

Air and sea

Spain has 110 airports. People can fly from one city to another, and to other countries. Spain also has several big ports and a large fleet of ships. These ships carry goods to and from the rest of the world.

Web Search ▶▶

▶ **www.renfe.es**
Spanish rail service.

▶ **www.iberia.com**
Iberia, the national airline.

▶ **www.trasmediterranea.es**
Ferries between Spain and the Balearic islands.

Education

Almost everyone in Spain can read and write. This is because schools are free and everyone has to go to school between the ages of six and 16.

School day

Children go to school from Monday to Friday. Most schools start at 9 A.M. and finish at 5 P.M. There is a break of about two hours when children usually eat their main meal of the day.

Below. **A class in a state primary school in Madrid.**

Left. Primary school children getting on a bus to go on an outing.

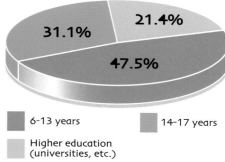

31.1% 21.4% 47.5%

■ 6-13 years	■ 14-17 years
■ Higher education (universities, etc.)	

Above. The number of children in education.

Kinds of school

Before the age of six, children may go to a preschool. After primary school, at age 12, they move to secondary school. About one-third of Spanish children go to private primary and secondary schools, for which their parents pay school fees.

Further education

After secondary school, some students go to upper secondary school or training centers. There they study for diplomas that allow them to go to technical college or university.

Foreign Languages

Most Spanish children learn to speak English or French at school. Some schools teach German, too. Many Spanish students go to other countries for part of their university course.

Web Search ►►

► http://unstats.un.org/unsd/demographic/products/socind/illiteracy.htm
Type Spain into the search engine for information and statistics about Spain.

Sports and Leisure

Spain's favorite sport is soccer, but golf, tennis, basketball, and fishing are popular, too. In 1992, the Olympic Games were held in Barcelona.

Sport

Spain's two main soccer clubs are Real Madrid and FC Barcelona. Real Madrid has won the European Championship nine times. Spain's warm climate means that golf and tennis are played all year round. Spanish golfers Jose Maria Olazabal and Severiano Ballesteros have won many major international tournaments.

Bullfighting

Most towns have a bullring, where crowds watch matadors fight and kill bulls. Bull-fighting is seen as a form of art. However, many people believe bullfighting is cruel and should stopped.

Below. **A matador in action at a bullring in Seville.**

Fiestas

Every city, town, and village in Spain has at least one fiesta, or festival. Many of them are held on holy days. People parade through the streets and fireworks are lit.

One famous fiesta is held in Pamplona. During the festival, bulls are let loose in the streets of the town. People watch from a safe place as a crowd of young men test their courage by running ahead of the bulls.

Pelota

The game of pelota is especially popular. It is played all over Spain and in other countries of the world. Players wear a wicker scoop on one arm to catch the ball and fling it back to another player or against the wall of the pelota court.

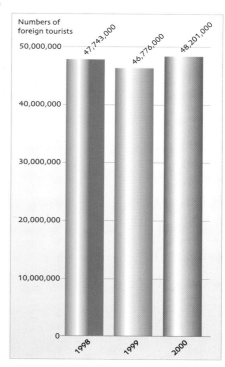

Numbers of foreign tourists

50,000,000
40,000,000
30,000,000
20,000,000
10,000,000
0

47,743,000   46,776,000   48,201,000

1998   1999   2000

Above. **Tourists visiting Spain in recent years.**

Below. **A basketball game in the Olympic hall in Barcelona.**

Web Search ▶▶

▶ **www.realmadrid.com**
Real Madrid soccer club.

▶ **http://www.fipv.net/eng/inicio/index.htm**
The game of pelota.

▶ **www.red2000.com/spain/toros**
The history of bullfighting.

21

Above. **Preparations for a festival parade in Barcelona.**

Tapas and Paella

Spanish people like to eat out in restaurants and bars. Bars often offer *tapas*. These are small snacks, such as pieces of fish, meat, and vegetables. *Paella* is a well known Spanish dish. It is a mixture of rice, meat, and different kinds of seafood.

Right. **An Easter week procession in Almería.**

Daily Life and Religion

Lunch is an important part of daily life in Spain. The working day finishes later than in most other countries.

Siesta

Most people in Spain have a long break in the middle of the day, called the siesta. The siesta allows people to rest during the hottest part of the day and to have a meal. Shops often close during the siesta but stay open in the evening until 8 or 9 P.M.

Religion

Most Spaniards are Roman Catholics but they do not go to church regularly. Until 1978, Roman Catholicism was the official religion. Then a new law broke the link between the state and the church. There are also Jews and Muslims living in Spain.

Muslim past

The south of Spain was once a Muslim country. Muslims are followers of the religion Islam. In cities such as Granada beautiful Islamic buildings can still be seen.

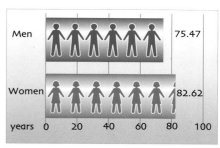

Above. **Average age Spanish people live to.**

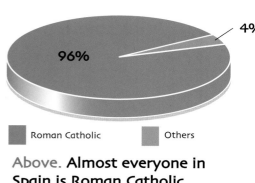

Roman Catholic   Others

Above. **Almost everyone in Spain is Roman Catholic.**

Web Search ▶▶

▶ www.alhambra-patronato.es
The Alhambra Palace, Granada.

▶ www.alhambra-patronato.es/
ingles/inforgenrl/informain.
htm
Food, drink, fiestas, and traditions in Spain.

Arts and Media

There are many famous Spanish artists, writers, architects, and musicians. They have created a rich culture that mixes the past and present.

Artists

Pablo Picasso is a world famous artist. Spain's many national museums and art galleries, such as the popular Museo del Prado in Madrid, display paintings by him and other Spanish artists, including Joan Miró, Salvador Dalí, Velázquez, and Goya.

Gaudí

Some of the most dramatic buildings in Spain were designed by the Spanish architect Antonio Gaudí (1852-1926). His best known work is the unfinished church *Sagrada Familia* (Holy Family) in Barcelona shown on the cover of this book.

Movies

Spain has a thriving movie industry. In the 1960s and 70s Spanish filmmakers, such as Luis Buñuel, produced many films that secretly criticized Franco, the dictator of Spain at that time. Today, Spanish directors work with Hollywood stars such as Nicole Kidman.

Right. **Flamenco dancers in Jerez.**

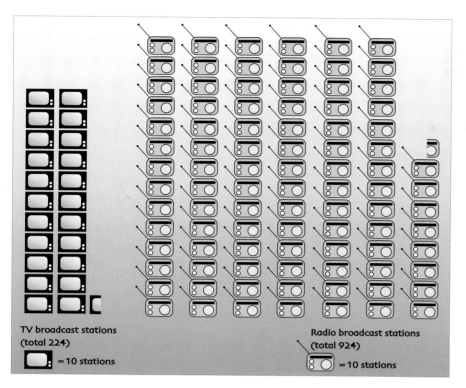

TV broadcast stations
(total 224)

⬛ = 10 stations

 Radio broadcast stations
(total 924)

= 10 stations

Above. Numbers of TV and radio stations in Spain.

Right. The Guggenheim Museum of Modern Art in Bilbao. This amazing building is covered in metal sheets.

Musicians and writers

Music is part of Spanish life. Today, Spain has its own rock bands and Latin American-style singers. Enrique Iglesias is an international star. Flamenco is a lively style of dancing from the south of Spain.

One of Spain's best-known novels is *Don Quixote*, written by Miguel de Cervantes between about 1605 and 1615. It tells the story of the knight Don Quixote and his sidekick, Sancho Panza.

Web Search ►►

► http://museoprado.mcu.es/
Prado Museum, Madrid.

► www.salvador-dali.org/
Salvador Dalí and museums with examples of his work.

► www.guggenheim-bilbao.es/
idioma.htm
The Guggenheim Museum in Bilbao.

► www.spanish-fiestas.com/
traditional/spanish-
flamenco-dancing.htm
The story of flamenco dancing.

Government

Spain is a monarchy, but real power lies with the government that is elected by the Spanish people.

The government in history

During the 1930s, Spain was taken over by its army, led by the dictator General Franco. After Franco died in 1975, the royal family was welcomed back to Spain and a government was elected.

 ETA

ETA is a political group that wants the Basque region in the north to be independent from the rest of Spain. ETA began a campaign of violence in the 1960s. After successful peace talks in the 1990s there was a ceasefire, but ETA returned to violence in 2000. The group has been blamed for a number of recent bombings.

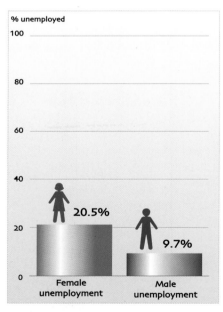

Above. **Adults without jobs.**

Spain is divided into 17 regions. Each region has its own independent local government.

Spain's Regions

Above. **Guards stand outside a government ministry building in the center of Madrid.**

Monarchy and the Cortes

In 1975, King Juan Carlos I became the head of state and the commander-in-chief of the armed forces.

The country is governed by the Cortes Generales, or parliament. It is made up of two parts, known as houses. They are called the Congress of Deputies and the Senate. The Congress of Deputies is more powerful than the Senate. It has 300 to 400 deputies, who are elected by the Spanish people. In the Senate, only 80 percent of the 259 senators are elected. The rest are appointed by the regional governments.

Web Search ►►

► www.casareal.es/
Information about Spain's king and royal family.

► http://www.congreso.es/
portal/page/portal/
Congreso/Congreso
The Congress of Deputies.

► www.senado.es/home_i.
html
Information about the Senate.

DATABASE

Historical Events: 300 B.C.E. to C.E. 1600

228 B.C.E Carthaginians conquer the south and east of Spain

206 B.C.E Spain becomes part of the Roman empire

C.E 415 The Visigoths invade Spain

711 Muslim Arabs from North Africa defeat the Visigoths

1212 Christian armies defeat Muslim forces

1469 Ferdinand II marries Isabella I, uniting Aragon and Castille

1492 The last Muslim stronghold of Granada is captured by Spanish Christians

1521 Explorer Hernán Cortés conquers Mexico

1533 Explorer Francisco Pizarro conquers Peru

1588 The Spanish king, Philip II, sends an armada to invade England. It is defeated by England's navy

Place in the World

During General Franco's rule, Spain was ignored by other countries. Since Franco's death, Spain has joined the European Union (EU) and many other international organizations.

Trade

Spain joined the EU in 1986. Most of its trade is with other countries in Europe. Spain also has close links with many South and Central American countries, especially Chile, Argentina, and Mexico. These countries were once part of Spain's empire.

Morocco

For many years, Spain and Morocco have disgreed over which of them should rule the small islands and territories off and on the coast of Morocco.

Gibraltar

Spain also claims ownership of the British territory of Gibraltar on the southern tip of the country. In 1967, the people of Gibraltar voted to remain British. In 2002, Britain and Spain discussed the idea of sharing Gibraltar, but no decision has since been made.

Below. **Every year the beaches around Alicante are crowded with tourists.**

Columbus

In 1492, Spain paid the explorer Christopher Columbus to sail west in the hope of reaching China. Instead, he landed in America.

Below. **Spain's imports and exports.**

EXPORTS
$160 billion (Machinery, motor vehicles, foodstuffs, consumer goods.

IMPORTS
$204 billion (Machinery and equipment, fuels, chemicals, semi-finished goods, foods, consumer goods)

 Web Search ▶▶

▶ http://news.bbc.co.uk/1/hi/ world/europe/992004.stm Timeline of modern Spain starting from the 1930s.

DATABASE

Historical Events from C.E 1600

1607 Madrid is made the capital of Spain

1701 War of Spanish Succession begins when the king dies childless

1714 War of Spanish Succession ends with Philip V as king

1821 Spain gives independence to Mexico

1824 Spain defeated in Peru, ending Spanish rule in South America

1898 Spain loses control of Cuba, Puerto Rico, and the Philippines

1936-39 Military takes over and civil war brings General Franco to power

1975 Franco dies. King Juan Carlos I crowned

1986 Spain joins the EU

1992 Barcelona hosts Summer Olympics

2003 Spain helps in war in Iraq

2004 Terrorist attack in Madrid prompts Spain to pull out of war in Iraq

Area:
194,900 sq miles
(504,784 sq km)

Population:
40,546,000

Capital city:
Madrid
(Population 5,050,000)

Other major cities:
Barcelona (pop. 1,635,000)
Valencia (pop. 765,000)
Sevilla (pop. 715,000)

Longest rivers:
Tagus (Tajo) (625 miles/
1,007 km)
Ebro (565 miles/910 km)
Duero (556 miles/895 km)

**Highest mountain on
Spanish mainland:**
Mulhacén (11,420ft/3,481m)

Currency:
euro

Flag:
A band of yellow with
bands of red above and
below. The national coat of
arms is on the left side of
the yellow band.

Languages:
Castilian (official language),
Catalan, Galician, Euskera
(Basque). Castilian is spoken
by most of the population

Major resources:
Coal, lignite, gypsum, iron
ore, alumina, sulfur, pumice,
feldspar, uranium, lead,
magnesite, zinc, fluorspar,
strontium, barite, peat,
copper, mercury, timber

Major exports:
Machinery, motor vehicles,
textiles, foods, consumer
goods, iron, and steel

**National holidays and
festivals:**
January 1: New Year's Day
January 6: Epiphany
May 1: May Day
July 25: St. James's Day
August 15: Assumption
October 12: National Day
November 1: All Saints' Day
December 6: Constitution
  Day
December 8: Immaculate
  Conception
December 25: Christmas
  Day

Religions:
Spain is almost entirely
Roman Catholic

Key Words

ARMADA
A large fleet of warships.

ARMED FORCES
The army, navy, and air forces; also known as the military or military forces.

BORDER
Line that marks the edge of a country.

CLIMATE
The usual weather at different times of the year.

CROPS
Plants grown for food or for products to sell, such as wheat and rice.

CULTURE
The beliefs, ideas, and customs of a group of people.

DESCENDANTS
People related to families who lived a long time ago.

DICTATOR
A leader who holds all the power in a country.

ECONOMY
The business, industry, and trade of a country.

ELECTED
Chosen by voting.

EMPIRE
A group of countries ruled by a single country.

EXPORTED
When goods or products are sold to other countries.

GOVERNMENT
The group of people who manage a country.

GRAZING
Animals feeding on grass and shrubs in fields and open areas.

HUMID
Hot and damp.

IMPORTS
Goods or products bought from other countries.

MANUFACTURING
Making large numbers of the same things usually by machine.

MONARCHY
Country ruled by a king or queen.

PLATEAU
High, flat ground.

POPULATION
All the people who live in a particular area.

RESOURCES
Materials that can be used to make goods or electricity, or to generate income for a country or region.

SERVICE INDUSTRY
Job that involves providing a service to other people.

TELECOMMUNICATIONS
Telephone, television, email, and other forms of electronic communications.

Index